THE BEST OF
BERGEN

Lotte Schønfelder

CONTENTS

The Ulriken cable-car.

MOUNTAINS AND FJORDS

Bergen is known as "The City Between Seven Mountains". Now, however, it has also become the proud bearer of the name "The City Between Seven Fjords" – a change which came about in 1972 when the administrative region of Bergen was merged with four surrounding districts to become the district of Bergen in the administrative region of Hordaland.

"It's crowded here in among the mountains" a Bergen poet once wrote – and it did get crowded! The city's population figures increased steadily over the centuries, partly due to an influx of outsiders, not least the Hansas. The city grew from the eastern side of Vågen round to the west and southwards down the valley. There, after the last war, new

parts of the city were built – it was, after all, getting rather cramped in the old city. 1955 saw Bergen breaking southwestwards through the mountains into the area of Fyllingsdalen. It was touch and go as to whether it would remain Norway's second largest city, but then came 1972 with its administrative reorganisation and the figures doubled!

will come as a surprise to many to hear that a good 40% of Bergen's 465 square kilometres is wooded, with the mountains making up 21%. But it is the mountains and fjords which have shaped Bergen, and which are the subject of innumerable songs. The sea was a source of trade and a link with the rest of the world – a world beyond, which the people of Bergen were

more in touch with than other parts of Norway. Geographically, the city turned its back on the rest of the country – only with the opening of the Bergen railway in 1909 did it really become part of Norway. The mountains which until then had closed off the city became public areas – in the old days as grazing land, more recently as a source of recreation. The

locals don't have far to go to get out into the country, and even less so these days. 1918 saw the opening of Fløibanen, the funicular railway running up to the top of Mount Fløyen – just as much a link to the suburbs for those living on the mountainside as a means of transport for walkers heading for the city's most popular mountain, also one of Bergen's

biggest tourist attractions. Then came
Ulriksbanen in 1961, a cable car to the
city's highest and "sacred" mountain
and also something of a tourist attraction
in its own right. The views from the
top are magnificent and once up in the
mountains, walkers have a wonderful
variety of walks and paths to choose from.

From Fløyen there are fantastic views of the city.

Bryggen with Fløyen in the background.

ALIVE WITH THE PAST

Bergen is immediately identifiable by its profile - the pointed gables of Bryggen. Included on UNESCO's World Heritage List, Bryggen was once the heart (not to mention the stomach) of the city and, together with Vågsbunnen, forms the oldest part of Bergen. Nevertheless, it's very much alive and kicking!

During the Middle Ages Bryggen stretched from where the Korskirken church now stands down as far as Bergenhus. Later the area was shortened and widened as Vågen was filled in and new quays were built. Bryggen's houses were designed to ensure that most of them could have their own stretch of shore. That's how things stood when the hanseatic merchants arrived, and that's how they still stand, though these days Bryggen's wooden houses date back no further than 1702 when a fire razed most of Bergen to the ground. However, the houses were rebuilt as exact replicas, and those which were ravaged by two fires in the 1950s were also rebuilt as careful copies. The only thing to have changed is the most southern area where, at the

beginning of the century, the people of Bergen managed to agree on a new district plan, tore down the wooden houses and replaced them with tall brick houses. But with the pointed gables facing the sea, retaining Bergen's profile.

Trading is still a way of life on Bryggen, though dried fish is decidedly less popular! These days the colourful line of buildings houses an abundance of small shops, restaurants, craftsmen, galleries and even a small museum. Anyone interested in finding out how Bergen's forefathers lived should visit the Hanseatic Museum at the southern end and the Schøtstuene assembly rooms behind Bryggen. Here is a chance to see how merchants and their servants lived day to day, and delve into their social comings and goings.

Bryggen has seen many an excavation project and some of the finds are on show in the Bryggen Museum to the north of the wooden houses, a centre for medieval archaeology. This area is also home to the Mariakirken church which, dating back to the twelfth century, is Bergen's oldest

preserved building. In the Middle Ages Bergen had a wealth of churches, but only three have survived: the Domkirken (Cathedral), the Korskirken and the Mariakirken, which is the best preserved, the other two being considerably altered over the centuries. The hanseatic merchants took over the Mariakirken for their own use and furnished it richly – a

late Gothic wooden altar from the end of the fifteenth century and a magnificent Baroque pulpit donated to the church in 1676.

A little further west lies Holmen, Norway's power centre in the twelfth and thirteenth centuries, today known as Bergenhus. Even after the king had headed east to Oslo, Holmen remained

the ecclesiastical, secular and military centre of western Norway. The large Kristkirken and other smaller churches in the area are long gone, but the stone hall which Håkon Håkonsson built to celebrate his son Magnus' wedding and coronation in 1261, possibly with the help of English craftsmen, stands to this very day. In the Middle Ages the hall saw a

umber of coronations, royal weddings
d important political meetings, but was
en ravaged over time and ultimately
ed as a warehouse. 700 years after the
rst celebrations it was the subject of a
yal visit once more – by which time it
d been restored after the considerable
mage sustained in an explosion in
44, the worst catastrophe to strike

Bergen during the war. These days the
Håkonshall is the finest hall in Bergen
and is widely used for concerts.

The other striking stone building
in Bergenhus is the Rosenkrantz Tower,
named after Erik Rosenkrantz who was
the king's representative in Bergen in
the middle of the sixteenth century. He
converted Magnus Lagabøte's thirteenth

century fortress tower to a residence with
a Renaissance facade facing the city. The
canons at the top of the tower also faced
Bergen, pointing towards the hanseatic
traders who gradually lost their power,
thanks to the king's dynamic representatives.

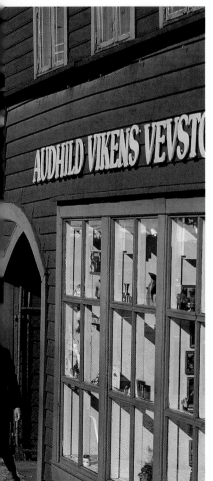

The narrow alleys of Bryggen.

Schøtstuene, the 16th/17th-century Hanseatic Assembly Rooms on Brygge[n]

HANSEATIC CITY

Bergen is sometimes referred to as a hanseatic city. While not strictly true, this sounds undeniably grander than "office city" which is what it was for the Hanseatic League, the German association of merchants which dominated north European trade during the Middle Ages, and which also had contacts in the Mediterranean.

Bergen traded in a commodity which was increasingly in demand in thirteenth century Europe – dried fish from northern Norway. However, the Hansas gradually came to dominate, taking over more and more of the foreign trade in a complex political game where the kings initially tried to stem the power of the hanseatic merchants. To no avail – the merchants ended up with both privileges and a monopoly on the trade of dried fis[h] out of the city. From the middle of the fourteenth century the League set up an office in Bergen — one of the four main offices along with London, Novgorod and Bruges.

The hanseatic merchants initially rented houses on the Bryggen wharf, and then went on to buy them. This explains

Room in the Hanseatic Museum.

hy Bryggen is sometimes referred to as anseatic, though the houses were already here when the Germans arrived. Bryggen does not, in other words, have hanseatic origins. The merchants were based there or around 400 years, though their power and influence waned from the mid-1500s onwards. A selfgoverning, purely male society, they were not supposed to mingle with the locals —

nevertehless there was lots of wine, women and song in the stretch behind Bryggen. When the Hanseatic League's power came to an end, the merchants had the option of returning to their own country or settling in Norway — many chose the latter, the result being some of Bergen's "good old" families and names.

View from Vågen towards Fløyen and Ulriken.

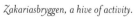
Zakariasbryggen, a hive of activity.

The old and the new meet.
The Dragon Boat Festival

Christian VII's monogram on the Old Town Hall recalls the king who was expected to visit but never came.

Håkonshallen, King Håkon Håkonsen's magnificent banqueting hall.

The Cathedral. *Mariakirken, dating back to the 12th century, is Bergen's oldest building.*
The tabernacle in Mariakirken (St Mary's Church) is one of Bergen's greatest ecclesiastical treasures.

FERSKVANNS-
KREPS
Kr. 40,-
pr ½ kg.

FERSK
SJØKREPS
Kr. 180,-
pr kg.

Arnfinn

Schweppes

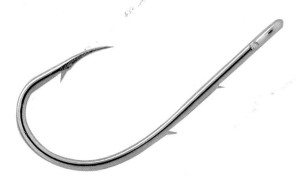

Bergen's famous fish market is an experience in itself.

Bergen Aquarium

FISH AND FORTIFICATION

With the exception of the Fantoft stave church, Edvard Grieg's home Troldhaugen and Ole Bull's island villa on Lysøen, everything in Bergen is within easy striking distance of the centre.

Many visitors begin at the city's fish market at Fisketorget where they are tempted by salmon, prawns, crabs and other delicacies from the deep. From

here it is but a hop, skip and a jump to the Fløibanen funicular railway, Bryggen, Bergenhus and the Mariakirken. And to the yellow bus which goes out to the delightful Gamle Bergen (Old Bergen) open air museum, just a ten minute drive away.

But other parts of the city centre are also worth investigating – a little to the

south lies Det Gamle Rådhus, the old city hall where the people's representatives have met since the middle of the 1500s. On the other side of the high-rise modern block which has been Bergen's City Hall since 1974 stands a large, whitewashed building: Manufakturhuset – Bergen's largest secular brick house in the Baroque style. Having started out as a

orkhouse, it now serves as council fices. Further south, in the small area f Marken, is the St. Jørgen Hospital. amed in 1409, it was, until recent mes, a hospital for lepers and had its wn church. As such, it is appropriate at it currently houses, among other ings, the world's only leprosy museum.

The Nordnes peninsula separates

Vågen from the Pudde Fjord, and has links with both fish and fortresses. At the very end of the peninsula is the Aquarium, one of Bergen's greatest attractions. Opened in 1960, it was financed by local fund-raising – nothing new to Bergen with its tradition of generous patrons and city folk who collect money for everything from the Maritime Museum and the

University Library to the Aquarium and the Grieghallen.

Nordnes is also home to Fredriksberg, a small fortress dating back to the 1660s, built after the 1665 battle between the English and the Dutch in Vågen, and also one of Bergen's former execution sites. Another part of the fortress is the Lavett houses, the old wooden houses near the

Aquarium. Fredriksberg was never actually used as a fortress but around 1820 it housed an observatory where Bergen's geographical location was determined.

The weather is not always fine in Bergen!

Grieghallen (concert hall). Inset: Gamlehaugen, Bergen's royal residence
King Harald and Queen Sonja arriving at the Bergen International Festival

CITY OF CULTURE

In a city where the title of "merchant" really meant something, it's hardly surprising that many an accusation has been levelled at the locals over the centuries for wrapping themselves up in their trading and shipping, dried fish and accounts.

Although there's no smoke without fire, the people of Bergen did actually see beyond their trading. Ever since the twelfth and thirteenth centuries when it was the capital of Norway, Bergen has attracted foreigners with the result that its merchants were not unaware of what was going on in Europe. They picked up on trends and ideas and were eventually rich enough to breathe life into these ideas. Sober in their day-to-day business, they really went to town elsewhere: building pavilions, designing gardens along foreign lines, enjoying music, reading, and indulging in the theatre.

1765 saw the foundation of "Musik-selskabet Harmonien", the origins of today's Bergen Philharmonic Orchestra, one of the oldest symphony orchestras in the world. In 1850 violin virtuoso and local lad Ole Bull founded Norway's first

ational theatre where both Henrik Ibsen
nd Bjørnstjerne Bjørnson cut their
ramatic teeth as playwrights and in-
ructors. Scandinavia's first major
omedy playwright, Ludvig Holberg,
pent most of his life in Copenhagen, but
as originally from Bergen and also wrote
famous book describing the city in his
ay. Norway's first important landscape

painter, J. C. Dahl, came from Bergen –
and the fact that Edvard Grieg was also a
local was the reasoning behind the Bergen
International Festival. Since the very first
festival in 1953, early summer in Bergen
has been transformed into what King Olav
in his time termed "a cultural Mecca" in
Norway. In other words the city has the
royal seal as a city of culture – and has also

been given the European seal as
European City of Culture for the year
2000.

Ole Bull's home on the island of Lysøen, in the neighbouring district of Os.

In 1885 Grieg purchased Troldhaugen, a
lovely Swiss-style villa on the shores of
Nordåsvannet. From then until his death,
Grieg spent every summer at Troldhaugen.

Interior view of Troldhaugen.

A Hardanger fiddle.

Edvard Grieg's music is a bridge betwe
Norway and Europe. His works represe
a blend of the European classical tradition and Norwegian folk music which v
unique in its day. Edvard Grieg was bo
in Bergen in 1843 and died in 1907

"Nina and Edvard Grieg at the piano". Painting by P.S. Krøyer, 1898.

Sheet of music, "The Death of Åse".

"Birch in Storm", J.C. Dahl, 1849.

ART MUSEUMS

Like every city, Bergen has its fair share
of museums and art collections. Two are,
however, unique: The Leprosy Museum
and the Buekorps Museum. The latter is
housed in Muren on Nordnes – a stone
building dating from the sixteenth century
resembling a town gate. The building
itself was originally used for celebrations
on the first floor and by farmers for

trading on the ground floor. The museum,
which is open at weekends, tells the story
of the city's buekorps, a type of boys'
brigade, which was set up in the middle
of the last century. These days the buekorps is a phenomenon confined to
Bergen, but has had offshoots in many
Norwegian cities.

Also unique – and impressive – is the

sizeable China collection at the Vestlandsk
Kunstindustrimuseum. The collection
of art, fabrics and other objects was
donated by Bergen General J. W. N.
Munthe who lived in China from 1887
and who, among other things, helped
modernise the Chinese army.

Another gift to Bergen was Rasmus
Meyer's collection of paintings, furniture

The boys' archery corps are a Bergen tradition.

d interiors which was housed in its own
ilding on Lille Lungegårdsvann, the
all lake in the centre of Bergen, in
24. At the heart of the collection lie
orwegian paintings spanning from J. C.
hl to Edvard Munch, who is represen-
d through many of his main works. The
llections also include rococo interiors
th their ceiling and wall paintings.

Bergen has also received donations from
people living outside the city, Rolf
Stenersen being one such patron – his
collection has been placed in Bergen
Billedgalleri and, of course, includes
paintings by the city's greatest painter
J. C. Dahl, for example the well-known
"Birch in a storm".

THE WOODEN CITY

While Bergen's archives boast an impressive collection of city plans, it is fire that has had more of an impact than any planners ever did. Apart from various public buildings made of stone, Bergen grew up over the centuries as a city of wooden buildings only to be devoured by fire at regular intervals. The worst was, perhaps, the great fire of 1702 which took most of the

city with it. The most expensive was the fire of 1916 – known as the Fire of Bergen – which razed the city centre to the ground from Murallmenningen to Christies Gate, coming to a halt just before the central fire station. By then it had destroyed so much that Bergen took on a whole new look in the 1920s.

But in former times the locals had a

tendency to ignore public orders and re build their wooden houses just as they h been before the fire. As such, some of th areas and streets of medieval Bergen hav been preserved, not least in Vågsbunner Elsewhere you will find wide streets de signed to slow down fire – without ever having much effect!

Despite its history of fires, Bergen is

ll one of Europe's largest wooden cities,
not the largest. Wooden houses wend
eir way up over Fjellsiden behind the
øibanen station, and clump together at
østet, in Skuteviken and Rosegrenden
Sandviken - to name but a few areas
here visitors can see houses as they were
days of yore. And even the smallest of
ouses were often inspired by the resi-

dences and pavilions of the wealthy, many
of which have survived to the present day.

All in all, Bergen is an exciting city for
those with an interest in architecture.
Passing the "Bergen empire", with its
wealth of detail, red-tiled roofs on white
houses, and historic stone and brick buildings, the walk from Kalfaret to Nordnes
and Sandviken is well worth taking.

Söre Steinkjellersmauet

UDSIGT ved DOMKIRKE GADEN og KORSKIRKE ALMINDING, BERGEN.

Domkirkegaten and Korskirkealmenningen. Watercolour by Johan F.L. Dreier, 1821.

"A Journeyman and an Assistant on the Hanseatic Wharf", water colours, Johan F.L. Dreier 1816.

En Svend og en Dreng paa den contoirske Bryjgge, i Staden Bergen.
Ein Gesell und ein Bursche auf der Brauerey, in der Stadt Bergen.
N.64.

"PRINCESS OF THE SEA"

Although Bergen may not literally have risen Aphrodite-like out of the waves, one of the city's many poets and song-writers described her as the "princess of the sea" — and it's not difficult to see why. The city was, in its way, born of the sea and has lived off the sea for well over 900 years.

The harbour is where it all started.

There were already settlers living along the water's edge when King Olav Kyrre decided to set up a "trading post" in 1070, thus founding what was to become Bergen — a name derived from the Norwegian words for "mountain" and "pasture". He chose to build his palace at the foot of Mount Ulriken — a spot easily accessible by long boat.

Bergen grew up along and around Vågen — and grew fast once it got going. Twelfth century Bergen developed into an important European trading centre, linking western and northern Norway with the rest of the world. It was a city wit a European feel, and even Norwegians outside Bergen have been known to acknowledge it as Norway's only city with

Watercolour by Johan F.L. Dreier, 1821

coherent city culture and tradition. A tradition which Bergen's citizens do their best to preserve.

Norway's first residential city and capital, Bergen went on over the centuries to become the largest city in Norway and indeed the Nordic Countries. Holmen, today's Bergenshus, attracted kings, armies and bishops in their time. Norway's poli-tical centre, this was also where Håkon Håkonsson had a huge stone hall built to celebrate the marriage and coronation of his son Magnus, an impressive building both then and now. The self-same Magnus later became known as Magnus Lagabøte (Magnus the Lawmaker), and his city law of 1276 became something of a model for others to copy.

Bergen has had its ups and downs over the centuries. Even though the king moved the capital to Oslo and the good times came and went, the city managed to retain its position as a maritime, trading and cultural centre – a city that's just a little bit different, populated by people who like to be a little bit different from other Norwegians.

The legend (top left):

A. Daß Schloß.
B. Ritterdetch.
C. S. Marien, Der Teutschen kauſleut kirch.
D. Der Residirender Ameer Stett behauſing.
   Die Brugk oder Contor genant.
E. Der Teutsche kauſleut Rhotſtube vnd borſe.
F. S. Halwrÿ, ain Vercreuſt.
G. S. Martini.
H. Ingangk der Stat von der Teutschen brugk.
I. Ad S. Crucem.
K. Thumbkirch vnd Schule.
L. Huſſital von den Teutschen.
M. Spittal der Stat.
N. Die alite kirsh, vrbis Carcer.
O. Der Stat kalck.
P. Ein garten teich.
Q. Der Stat marckt, vormals.
R. Die Wage, flu.Pontis & Oppidi portus.
S. Deß Bischoffs garte.
T. Erichs Roſenkrantz garte.
V. S. Iohanns wall.
X. Die ſwarte, Ventorum index.

Hieronymus Scholeus sua manu descripsit

BERGA NOORWEGIÆ

The Scholeus Print. The oldest and best-known view of Bergen was drawn by Hieronimus Scholeus and etched in copper by Franz Hogenberg. It occupied a double page in a book published in 1588, one of a series of six volumes issued between 1572 and 1618. The Scholeus Print was to remain the international image of Bergen for almost 200 years.

GUILDS AND LEARNING

In the beginning were shipping and trading. Although home to the kings of Norway, Bergen did not have a large and rich hinterland and its people worked as traders (importing and exporting) and craftsmen. As such, the city catered not only for tradesmen, ship-owners and sailors, but also for craftsmen. Specialists in their various fields, the latter had their own areas and quarters in the city and formed their own guilds. The oldest of the Norwegian guilds is the Bergen Goldsmiths' Guild which dates back to 1568, with the bakers following suit not long after. Bergen is still a city rich in craft traditions – not least in terms of goldsmiths and bakers!

But a city cannot live by trade alone.

These days Bergen is just as much a centre of learning as a centre of commerce, though trade in fish oil has made way for North Sea oil. Established a little after the last world war, Bergen's university builds on traditions from the Bergen Museum, founded in 1825. The city is also home to Norway's first business school which still enjoys a prestigious reputation; the

Hanseatic cog, 1500.

Directorate of Fisheries and its Institute of Marine Research; a college of art, craft and design; colleges of engineering and education; a music academy; the internationally recognised Christian Michelsen Institute; and a high technology centre with its diverse range of activities. It was also where the renowned Bergen school of meteorologists came into being.

In the old days the people of Bergen sent their children abroad to get an education and learn about crafts and trading. These days Bergen can teach foreigners a thing or two!

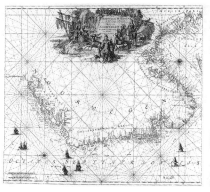

Dutch map, probably 18th-century.

Flåmsdalen and the Flåm Railway, a branch of the Bergen Line. Above: Tvindefossen waterfall.

GATEWAY TO THE FJORDS

When in Rome, do as the Romans do. And when in Bergen, make sure you take a trip out into the fjords! It's not for nothing that Bergen has been termed "Fjord Capital" and "Gateway to the Fjords". The city is ideally positioned between the majesty of the Sogne Fjord and the charm of the Hardanger Fjord. During the summer months there is a veritable exodus of cruises heading both north and south, and closer in to Bergen are countless smaller fjords and islands – a paradise

The Aurland Fjord.

or boating folk. The Sogne Fjord is the world's longest and deepest fjord, while Hardanger's glaciers, waterfalls and mountains have inspired many an artist.

Even mere mortals like ourselves can wax lyrical when the fruit trees blossom their way down almost to the water's edge while snow still glistens atop the distant peaks…

The Nærøy Fjor

Bondhus Glacier.

Låtefoss waterfal

Above: Steindalsfossen waterfall. Below: Vøringsfossen waterfall.

© Scandinavian Film Group A/S
Waldemar Thranesgt. 77
N-0175 OSLO

E-mail: sfg@sn.no
Tel: +47 22 20 84 02
Fax: +47 22 20 70 39

Author: Lotte Schønfelder
Design: Bergsnov, Mellbye & Rosenbaum as
Printed by: Tangen Grafiske Senter A/S
Translation: Berlitz A/S

Captions for full-page illustrations:
Page 1. Statsraad Lehmkuhl, Bergen's magnificent sailing
vessel, moored at Bryggen.
Pages 2-3. Bergen city centre.
Pages 4-5. Old Bergen.
Pages 6-7. Bryggen with Fløyen in the background.
Pages 60-61. Otternes village square, Aurland.
Page 64. The blossoming orchards of Hardanger.

Photographers:
Top = A
Top left = B
Top right = C
Bottom = D
Bottom left = E
Bottom right = F

Samfoto:
Bård Løken: 58D, 59, 60-61, 62D, 63A, 64.
Jørn Areklett Omre: 32DE, 52A, 58B.
Pål Hermansen: 20-21A, 52E, 53D, 62A, 63D.
Helge Sunde: 11BF, 40B, 43F, 49A, 52F.
J.B. Olsen: 12EF, 62C.
Stig Tronvold: 62B.

Willy Haraldsen: 1, 4-5, 6-7, 12F, 16-17A, 18EF, 22A, 25D,
26F, 29F, 32B, 36-37, 39F, 43A, 44A, 45EF, 50B.
Per Eide; 8CEF, 12A, 13, 14-15, 17D, 19, 21F, 22D, 23A,
26B,27EF, 29AE, 30A, 38AE, 39A, 41E, 42, 43E, 53AC.

Billedbyrået A/S:
Øystein Klakegg: 2-3, 8D, 38D, 44F, 50D.
Pål Hoff: 8A, 18, 27A, 28B, 29D, 38F, 40F.
O. Uthaug: 8, 33.
Robin Strand: 10, 11, 24-25, 38F, 41A.
Per Nybø: 38E, 41EF.
Harald Bjørnstad: 39, 38E, 39E.
R. Hjertholm: 31, 42C, 49.

Jon Fjeldstad: 23F.
O. Væring: 48.
Bergen Sjøfartsmuseum: 57DF.
Museet Lysøen: 44E.
Bergen Museum: 54 BE, 55, 56, 57A.
Statens Kunstmuser, Stockholm: 47A